FOSSILS:

Relics of the Classic Rock Era

Volume One: The '70s

Curated by Rev. Keith A. Gordon

!@#
EXCITABLE
PRESS

New York · Nashville

Fossils: Relics of the Classic Rock Era

ISBN #978-1540682796

Copyright 2016 by Rev. Keith A. Gordon & Excitable Press

Published by Excitable Press, A Conspiracy M.E.D.I.A company
35 Montclair Ave, Batavia NY 14020

Find us on the web @ www.thatdevilmusic.com

ACKNOWLEDGEMENTS

All advertising artwork herein courtesy of the respective record labels.

Cover photograph by Clarita, courtesy of Morguefile.com

THANX to Martin Popoff for inspiring *Fossils* both in conversation and with his tireless work ethic (really, have you seen how many books this guy's written? Makes the rest of us rockcrit types look like slackers!)

MUCH GRATITUDE to all who have helped, supported, or just merely tolerated my writing and publishing efforts through the years: Brother Willie Jemison, Steve Morley, Fred Mills, Thom King, Threk Michaels, Bill Claypool, Sharon Underwood and, of course, my lovely wife Tracey, without whose patience none of this would ever happen!

THANX also to those "O.G.'s" of rock criticism, "Ranger" Rick Johnson and Lester Bangs, for their original inspiration, and to folks like Bill Knight, Dave Marsh, Bill Holdship, John Kordosh, Robert Haber, Cary Baker, Mark Pucci, Bruce Iglauer, Ken Bays, Art Tipaldi, and Henry Yates for aiding and abetting my efforts throughout the decades...

BUY MY BOOKS! From the Reverend's pen: *The Other Side of Nashville*, the "incomplete history & discography of the Nashville rock underground, 1976-2006;" *Let It Rock!*, a collection of rock album reviews; *Rollin' 'n' Tumblin'*, a collection of blues album reviews; and many more can be found on Amazon.com or That Devil Music.com!

Introduction: Classic Rock Relics

It's no secret that the Reverend was bitten by the rock 'n' roll bug at an early age. As a pre-teen, I lived off the sounds on the radio and the few rockin' 45s that I purchased with my meager allowance. I graduated to full-length albums in my early teens once I learned that a few stolen hubcaps would earn me the cash to buy that new LP I coveted.

My first rock album purchase was Grand Funk Railroad's *Live*, bought on sale for $3.33 at a local shop in Erie, Pennsylvania. The obsession only grew from there, and the record collection grew rapidly from both my ill-gotten financial gains and numerous (and frequently unpaid) memberships in mail-order record clubs.

Before I'd even bought my first vinyl, however, I was addicted to music magazines dedicated to the genre – which meant the quarter-fold tabloid *Rock* magazine (often featuring writing by Dave Marsh and Patti Smith, two early faves), *Rolling Stone*, and *Crawdaddy* at first; later I jumped headfirst into *Creem, Zoo World, Trouser Press*, and *Bomp!*

To my young, impressionable mind, the ads for new albums published by these zines were often as exotic and intoxicating as the records themselves (and besides, I'd never hear even half the records I saw advertised). I'd dissect album ads, learning about new bands, and match up what the ads copy stated alongside the record reviews in the back of each rag. I soon found myself buying double copies of my favorite zines and carefully extracted ads that I liked to tack on my bedroom wall (my own "Sanctum Sanctorum," as it were).

The practice continued when I literally fled my parent's abode at age eighteen to share an apartment with a biker buddy, my favorite ads adorning the wall of my room alongside my treasured Pioneer sound system and reel-to-reel recorder. At some point, the ads came down from the wall and were lost to time, as were many of the magazines (the bulk of which were stolen by a cretin nicknamed "Skipper," upon which I will one day wreak a horrible vengeance). Life went on, as it is wont to do…

Now on the doddering downslide of middle age, I still find myself fascinated by old music magazines and the ads therein. I've been writing about rock 'n' roll for nearly 45 years at this point, writing – literally –

Introduction: Classic Rock Relics

thousands of LP reviews and yet I still find ads for albums I've never seen or heard in these ragged old zines. Several discussions with friend and colleague Martin Popoff provided the inspiration for *Fossils*, and while he may yet perform his own archeological 'dig' into antiquated album advertising, this is my own personal trip into our cultural past.

Within these pages, I dissect and comment on nearly four-dozen vintage album ads, providing some band history and my own view of what worked, artistically, and what, in retrospect, failed in these ads of yore. I understand that this is a rather arcane corner of rock 'n' roll history, with all the dust and cobwebs that such applies, but I'm hoping that some readers – not just Martin and I – find some magic in these "classic rock relics."

Rev. Keith A. Gordon
November 2016
Somewhere outside of Buffalo, New York in the heart of the 'Rust Belt'

Email the Reverend: thatdevilmusic.com@gmail.com

Contents

AC/DC's *Let There Be Rock* (1977)

Save for a few gas-huffing, head-banging hard rock fans, America didn't really discover Australia's AC/DC until the band's 1979 album *Highway To Hell*, the first of three red-hot, high-charting LPs produced by Robert "Mutt" Lange (including 1980's blockbuster, ten-times-platinum pancake *Back In Black*). *Let There Be Rock* was the band's fourth album, and the first to see international release (AC/DC's first two Aussie efforts were released stateside in 1976 as *High Voltage*, whereas the band's legitimate third album, *Dirty Deeds Done Dirt Cheap*, wasn't released in the U.S. until 1981, by which time AC/DC had become bona fide world-beaters).

Let There Be Rock is also, perhaps, the best representation of the band's original line-up, with leather-lunged singer Bon Scott and bassist Mark Evans alongside guitarists Angus and Malcolm Young and drummer Phil Rudd. Building on the boogie-blues blueprint that the band adheres to, roughly, to this very day, *Let There Be Rock* offers up all of the typical AC/DC lyrical tropes, from sexual abandon ("Whole Lotta Rosie") and the joys of rock 'n' roll ("Let There Be Rock") to the sort of mindless, greasy, guitar-driven pomp 'n' boogie that has become the band's stock in trade ("Hell Ain't A Bad Place To Be," "Problem Child"). Although the album would only graze the bottom quarter of the *Billboard* magazine Top 200 chart upon release (hitting #152), it has since gone double-platinum for an amazing two million+ Frisbees sold.

The label's ad for *Let There Be Rock* perfectly captured up the band's public image – lewd, crude, and sexually obsessive – which was also the agenda of the punters and miscreants that made up the band's target (i.e. teen and young adult) male audience.

Fossils: Relics of the Classic Rock Era

AC/DC's *Powerage* (1978)

If AC/DC's *Let There Be Rock* helped introduce the Australian hard rockers to American audiences, the band's 1978 outing *Powerage* wedged its foot in the door so that, a year later, *Highway To Hell* could barge in, re-arrange the furniture, and paint the walls with high-wire riffage. Ostensibly the band's fifth album (second released internationally), it was the first with acclaimed bassist Cliff Williams, who would play nearly 40 years with the gang before retiring in 2016, and it was the last album to be produced by the team of Vanda & Young ("Mutt" Lange would take over the board for *Highway*).

Although *Powerage* presented an uneven set of songs – understandable in that AC/DC had cranked out five full-length discs in four years – it still included long-lived original material like "Riff Raff," "Down Payment Blues," and "Rock 'n' Roll Damnation," all of which would become enduring fan favorites. Leather-lunged frontman Bon Scott came into his own with a stunning vocal performance that combined his whiskey-soaked grit with emotional power, and overall the entire band, from its playing to its songwriting, displayed a growing maturity that would help launch them to stardom.

Dubbing their sound "search and destroy rock 'n' roll," Atlantic Records' ad for the album showcased fiery, flamboyant guitarist Angus Young in full maniac schoolboy mode, a fitting image that would come to define the band in years to come. *Powerage* outperformed *Let It Rock* by an impressive twenty-one chart positions, but it would 'only' achieve Platinum™ album status, considered by many to be the 'lost album' of the band's early years.

A&M Records' *No Wave* ad (1979)

The record industry slipped into a bad sales slump during the late '70s – former chart-busting, world-beating bands were suffering from serious artistic fatigue, and punk's "class of '77" had largely fallen by the wayside, with only the Clash remaining serious contenders as the '70s gave way to the 1980s. If punk rock was the snarling, tooth-gnashing, hungry feral side of rock 'n' roll at the end of the decade, the corporate pigeonhole of "new wave" was the domesticated young pup that would happily sit at your feet, drooling and wagging its tail. The "new wave" marketing 'dream come true' never really caught on in the U.S. outside of a few bands, but it didn't stop the major labels from trying to exploit the whitewater currents of radical new sounds and fashion.

It could rightfully be said that A&M Records "won" the new wave rock gold rush, the label signing three commercially-successful acts in the Police (big win!), Joe Jackson, and Squeeze (originally labeled "U.K. Squeeze"). All three bands were included on *No Wave*, A&M's attempt to seem 'cool' and 'edgy,' an otherwise traditional record label sampler album gussied up in "new wave" sounds and images. A&M flooded the market with these pancakes and even sold copies of the album via mail order through ads like this one from *Trouser Press* circa 1979.

As these things go, the ad is fairly workmanlike – the raffish young punk with the era-appropriate skinny tie is balanced upon an ironing board, "surfing the new wave" you see, while the ad copy urged listeners to take "a musical dip into the ocean of contemporary sounds." The LP's track list included the aforementioned heavy hitters as well as tunes by Klark Kent (Sting's pre-Police band), the Stranglers (future U.K. punk legends), the Dickies (silly stateside punk), and the Secret, whoever the hell they were. Three different versions for sale, including blue colored vinyl (the rage at the time) and a limited edition, numbered black vinyl edition.

Duane Allman's *An Anthology* (1972)

Guitarist Duane Allman's tragic death in October 1971 not only left the Allman Brothers Band in disarray; it also robbed the rock 'n' roll world of a creative, innovative, and electrifying musician. Released roughly a year after the accident that took Allman's life, the two-disc set *An Anthology* smells like record label exploitation, a quick cash-in released not too soon after the subject's passing, but not so late that people would have forgotten. In reality, it was a public service on behalf of the label (tho' odds are they didn't view it that way…), providing fanboys such as your humble writer to discover other facets of Allman's talents that may not have been as well known as his band work.

Capricorn Records' advertising for *An Anthology* was simple but effective – the album's cover front and center, showing a shirtless Allman fishing in some funky swamp, and listing some of the artists the guitarist had played with that are represented by the track list. Allman had a reputation as a studio hot-shot, and he lent his talents to a slate of R&B legends, spicing up performances by giants like Wilson Pickett, Aretha Franklin, King Curtis, and Clarence Carter, all of whom are included on *An Anthology*.

An Anthology also includes a number of Allman's better-known Allman Brothers Band performances, songs like "Statesboro Blues" and "Little Martha" as well as rare early recordings by his band Hourglass, and rock 'n' roll session work with artists like Boz Scaggs (the amazing Fenton Robinson blues cover "Loan Me A Dime") and, of course "Layla," his legendary duet with Eric Clapton and Derek & the Dominos. *An Anthology* sold well enough to spawn a second volume two years later and, in 2013, a seven-CD box set titled *Skydog* that provided a final epitaph for a talent taken far too soon.

DUANE ALLMAN
an anthology

Duane Allman playing with Hourglass;
Clarence Carter; Wilson Pickett; Aretha Franklin; King Curtis;
John Hammond; Boz Scaggs; Delaney, Bonnie and Friends;
Eric Clapton; Derek and the Dominoes; and The Allman Brothers Band.
A Two Record Set Including a 20 Page Booklet.

Manufactured by Warner Bros. Records Inc.

Bad Company's *Straight Shooter* (1975)

British blues-rock outfit Bad Company already had a heady track record before the release of its 1974 self-titled debut album. Paul Rodgers, the voice of the band, put together Bad Company after the break-up of Free, his legendary 1960s-era outfit. Rodgers brought drummer Simon Kirke from that band along for the ride, joining guitarist Mick Ralphs from Mott the Hoople and bassist Boz Burrell from King Crimson to form Bad Company. The debut album's first hit single, "Can't Get Enough," hit #5 on the chart, pushing the album itself to number one.

A year later, Bad Company released *Straight Shooter*, more of the same hard rock and boogie blues that characterized the band's first effort – no surprise, really, as many of the songs had been written in '73 around the time of the debut (and may have been leftovers from those first sessions). The ad campaign for *Straight Shooter* showcases the band (and friends) gambling at a craps table (in keeping with the two dice theme on the album's cover, the dice showing a "natural" eleven), portraying Bad Company taking risks and living the rock 'n' roll lifestyle.

Sadly, *Straight Shooter* displayed none of the risk the ad was clearly trying to picture, the band following the same formula as the debut, and one that they're more or less chase throughout the remainder of the 1970s (or until Rodgers left the band). *Straight Shooter* was only slightly less successful than the debut, hitting #3 on the album chart on the strength of the hit single "Feel Like Makin' Love," which itself rose to #10, followed by "Good Lovin' Gone Bad," which was also a Top 40 hit single.

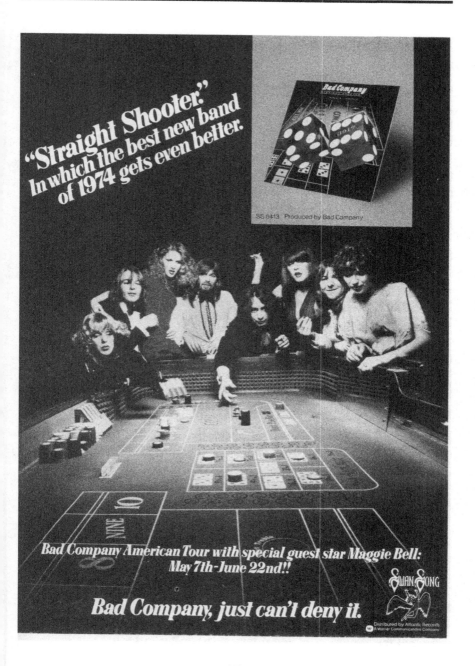

Blue Oyster Cult's *Some Enchanted Evening* (1978)

The decade of the 1970s was the era of the live rock 'n' roll album, with just about any old band of road warriors slapping a hastily-recorded show on vinyl and laughing all the way to the bank after picking their fans' wallets. The best-known of these concert trinkets was, perhaps, former Humble Pie guitarist Peter Frampton's 1976 set *Frampton Comes Alive!* When the obscure fretburner's budget-priced twofer hit the top of the charts, the race was on among major label A&R reps to break *their* pet band in a similar manner. Aerosmith, Thin Lizzy, Ted Nugent, and Led Zeppelin were among those to flog live sets in the wake of Frampton's chart breakthrough.

Blue Oyster Cult was ahead of the curve, the band releasing its first live set, *On Your Feet Or On Your Knees*, in 1975 – only three albums into its short career. The band's electrifying live chops obviously entertained the 'Iron Lung' set, and fans put aside their bongs long enough to drive the LP to #22 on the charts, BOC's best-selling flapjack to date. By the time of the release of *Some Enchanted Evening* in 1978, Blue Oyster Cult had racked up a pair of red-hot hitters in 1976's *Agents of Fortune* (#29) and the following year's *Spectres* (#43). The two albums vaulted BOC to the top of the arena-rock ranks, so the band was ripe for the release of another live set.

Some Enchanted Evening was a curiously unsatisfying curio, the album's too-brief set list featuring the two latest band hits in "(Don't Fear) The Reaper" and "Godzilla," accompanied by odd covers of the MC5's "Kick Out The Jams" and the Animals' "We Gotta Get Out Of This Place." No mind, though, 'cause the band's blockheaded fans (myself included) bought this thing by the truckload, driving it to #44 on the charts. The label's ad campaign for the album didn't really help anything…featuring the album cover's very cool depiction of the Reaper, the best concept the art department could come up with was "don't fear the Blue Oyster Cult," a play on the title of the band's best-known ditty. Any half dozen of the band's fans could have come up with something better, provided they were sober enough and not just sitting, staring at the album cover and saying "whoooaaa" after too much ganja.

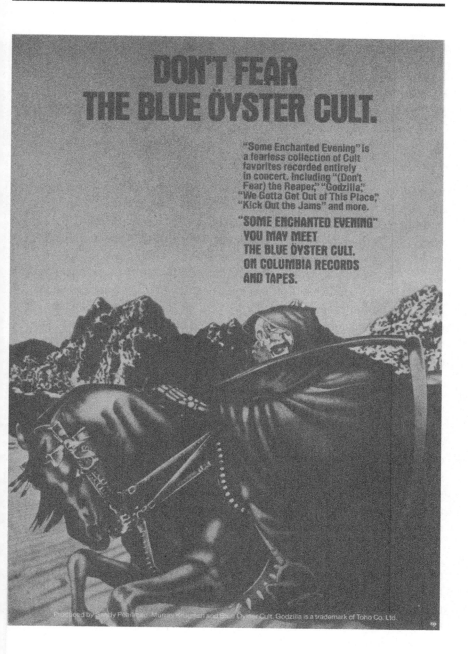

Boston's *Don't Look Back* (1978)

Boston's self-titled 1976 debut was a left-field success, taking the charts back for honest-to-god rock music from the dwindling ranks of prog-rock diddlers and self-flagellating 'Avocado Mafia' singer/songwriters. The album's first single, "More Than A Feeling," hit #5 on the chart, the album hitting #3 in the first of three times that it's charted on the *Billboard* 200 since its initial release.

It took Boston two years to come up with a suitable follow-up to their debut, a lifetime in those heady, mega-creative days of the 1970s (although barely a heartbeat compared to today's artists, who take two years just to figure out what clothes they're going to wear to the next awards show). *Don't Look Back* was nearly a carbon-copy of Boston's debut, Tom Scholz's electronically-enhanced fretwork fastidiously laid on tape by the notoriously obsessive artisan, singer Brad Delp's vocal phrasings and approach so similar as to think that these songs were recorded at the same time as the debut. The only visible difference can be found in the more retrospective nature of the lyrics, which show a band burdened by success.

The advertising for *Don't Look Back* that was whipped up by the obviously uninspired Epic Records art department didn't really have to do much more than announce the album's impending release. Featuring a different illustration of the uber-cool spaceship featured on the album's cover (itself reminding of a different rocket ship on the debut LP), the ad screams "it's here!" to the band's legion of fans. We subsequently showed up at our local record stores en masse, rolls of pennies in hand, to buy *Don't Look Back*, driving the album to numero uno on the chart, the band scoring another pair of hit singles.

Sadly, the great rock 'n' roll hope of the 1970s wouldn't release its third album for eight damn years, Boston's *Third Stage* the result of much blood, sweat, and tears on the part of Messrs. Scholz and Delp (the only two remaining original members). Some things just don't change, though, and *Third Stage* joined its fellow Boston albums in the ranks of multi-platinum sales blockbusters.

Jimmy Buffet's *A1A* (1974)

A1A, the fourth album from Jimmy Buffett, was a transitional work in every sense of the word. Buffett had spent better than half a decade in the trenches of Nashville trying to make it as a country singer and songwriter, playing dives like Sam's Pizza Place and pitching tunes to publishers on Music Row. Buffett's third ABC Dunhill album, 1974's *Living and Dying in 3/4 Time*, scored a minor pop and country hit in "Come Monday," an effective mid-tempo soft rocker closer in spirit to material from California 'Avocado Mafia' songwriters like Jackson Browne or David Crosby as opposed to the new brand of cosmic cowboy like Guy Clark or Jerry Jeff Walker.

In the wake of a divorce and re-location to Key West, Florida Buffett began to shed his Music City roots and re-invented himself as a country-rock beach bum. *A1A*, named for the highway which runs along the Atlantic coast of Florida, mixes autobiographical tunes like "Trying To Reason With Hurricane Season," "A Pirate Looks at Forty," and "Life Is Just A Tire Swing" with choice covers like Alex Harvey's "Makin' Music For Money" and John Sebastian's "Stories We Could Tell," the performances blending country, rock, and the occasional island riddims. Buffett enjoyed a minor country hit with the album's twangiest track, the humorous "Door Number Three" (#88), while the album itself struck a chord with mainstream audiences, *A1A* becoming the singer's highest-charting LP to date (#25).

The ABC Dunhill ad for *A1A* wasn't particularly effective or gripping, the giant head of Jimmy Buffett hovering, godlike, above a sand-coursed stretch of highway. The ad copy says little of the album save for an attempt to make a Nashville connection for the music – not the best way, perhaps, to sell the singer's new creative direction, but then again, ABC didn't have the spare cash to spread around and hype the album at the time. It didn't matter, really, 'cause Buffett had clearly found his musical blueprint and, after his tiny label was absorbed by the multinational MCA Records, he'd hit the big time three years later with his signature song "Margaritaville," the perfect distillation of his beach bum persona which would hit Top 20 on both the pop and country charts.

Canned Heat's *Future Blues* (1970)

It had been a long, strange trip for blues-rock stalwarts Canned Heat between the band's founding in 1966 and the 1970 release of *Future Blues*. Formed by blues fanatics Al Wilson and Bob "The Bear" Hite and named for an obscure blues song by an even more obscure Delta bluesman, Canned Heat had recorded four studio albums, enjoyed a couple of smash hit singles, and performed a knock-out live set at the Woodstock Festival in 1969.

For any other band, this modest commercial success and tradition-based blues-rock sound would have had rock's critical establishment hanging by their tails from the trees and throwing poo at anyone who dared dissent from the conventional wisdom. Oddly enough, however, Canned Heat never received much love from the scribes, the band somehow deemed "inauthentic" and/or "sell outs" by the rock 'n' roll press (in spite of their later collaboration with blues legend John Lee Hooker, a rigid taskmaster who didn't suffer fools lightly).

Regardless, the band had its fans, and *Future Blues* performed about as well as Canned Heat's previous efforts, scoring a minor Top 30 hit with a cover of Wilber Harrison's "Let's Work Together." The album itself inched its way up to #59 on the *Billboard* 200 chart...no mean feat, considering the band's blues obsession in the fledgling era of album oriented rock (AOR). The label's creative department did little but splash the album's cover art on the page with the "one small step for man" tagline, but the cover art itself was brilliant, if controversial.

Blending the iconic photo of the raising of the American flag over Iwo Jima during World War II with the recent (summer 1969) moon landing, it's as if the band was declaring both a new sense of musical freedom as well as commenting on the country's societal distress (thus the upside-down flag), no doubt in response to Al Wilson's growing environmental concerns. The cover perfectly captures the vibe of the band at the time. *Future Blues* would be the last album to feature band founder Wilson, who tragically passed away not long after its release.

Elvis Costello's *Armed Forces* (1978)

The 'angry young man of punk,' Elvis Costello was a moderately-successful recording artist by 1979, his only real connection to punk rock being the era in which he began his career (Costello came up through the early '70s pub-rock scene that led to punk), and the emotional strength of his whipsmart lyrics. Costello's third album, and second with top-notch backing band the Attractions, *Armed Services* proved to be the singer/songwriter's commercial breakthrough in the states, hitting number ten on the *Billboard* album charts and eventually earning Gold™ Record status (it hit number two on the U.K. charts).

Armed Forces originally had the working title *Emotional Fascism*, Costello writing a bunch of songs that use politics as a metaphor for personal relationships and romance. Although his lyrics are often overly-obtuse, songs like "Oliver's Army," "Accidents Will Happen," and "Two Little Hitlers" have endured because of Costello's maturing sense of melody and classic pop songwriting chops. Columbia Records seemingly had no idea how to promote *Armed Forces*, the art department delivering a rather perfunctory graphic that featured a big photo of Costello, a small photo of the album cover, and a banner hyping the free 7" three-song EP that came with the U.S. version of the album (*Live at Hollywood High* including sizzling versions of "Alison," "Watching The Detectives," and "Accidents Will Happen").

The album was a commercial success in spite of its meager ad campaign, but it also signaled the beginning of the end of Costello's commercial fortunes in the U.S. Subsequent album releases would sell fewer and fewer copies stateside, making Costello a cult artist with a great legacy but only modest sales.

Rick Derringer's *If I Weren't So Romantic, I'd Shoot You* (1978)

Singer, songwriter, and guitarist Rick Derringer made his bones as the frontman of the McCoys, whose lone chart-topping hit "Hang On Sloopy" led to opening for the Rolling Stones during their 1966 U.S. tour and certain immortality on oldies compilation albums. Derringer moved on from his teen idol years with a successful solo career ("Rock and Roll Hoochie Koo") and a long tenure playing with, and producing albums for Johnny Winter and the Edgar Winter Group. By mid-decade, the guitarist had formed a band with rock 'n' roll veteran Kenny Aaronson (Dust, Stories) on bass and rookie Vinny Appice (future Black Sabbath and Dio) on drums in a band simply called 'Derringer.'

Derringer released a pair of well-received albums in 1976's self-titled debut and the following year's *Sweet Evil*, an album my colleague Martin Popoff calls "a rock-solid classic from American metal's early days" in his *The Collector's Guide to Heavy Metal, Volume 1: The Seventies* book. Neither album sold particularly well, though, so changes were afoot – Myron Grombacher took over the drum seat, former Edgar Winter Group vocalist Dan Hartman was brought in to handle the singing, and Derringer collaborated with artists like Alice Cooper and Patti Smith on the songwriting.

The Blue Sky/CBS Records ad for Derringer's third album, *If I Weren't So Romantic, I'd Shoot You*, hypes these collaborations as well as the band's cover of Warren Zevon's "Lawyers, Guns and Money" for what may be one of the worst album titles, ever. The ad is oddly effective, utilizing the circular target graphic from the album cover behind a photo of the band joyfully pointing finger guns at the viewer.

Although the ad displays a roguish élan, it was too little, too late as *If I Weren't So Romantic* went nowhere fast, and Rick Derringer returned to his solo career with 1979's acclaimed *Guitars and Women*, produced by his buddy Todd Rundgren. Although *If I Weren't So Romantic* found little commercial or critical acceptance at the time, in retrospect critics like Popoff have called the album "another sumptuous classic from one of rock's unsung session and solo men…"

The New Derringer.
You'll love it so much it'll hurt.

Derringer's album features new Rick Derringer collaborations with Alice Cooper, Bernie Taupin, Patti Smith, Derringer's new version of Warren Zevon's "Lawyers, Guns and Money" and new songs from the band.

DERRINGER
IF I WEREN'T SO ROMANTIC, I'D SHOOT YOU
including
It Ain't Funny/Midnight Road
Lawyers, Guns And Money/Power Of Love/EZ Action

"If I Weren't So Romantic, I'd Shoot You." It's the best Derringer yet. On Blue Sky Records and Tapes.

Produced by Mike Chapman.
Blue Sky is a trademark of Blue Sky Records, Inc. Distributed by CBS Records.

© 1978 CBS Inc.

Devo's *Q: Are We Not Men? A: We are Devo!* (1978)

Only in the heady 1970s could a label (Warner Brothers, in this instance) wager on such an unlikely act and pull off a commercial coup. Devo arose from the ranks of the indie punk/new wave scene with a striking visual image (yellow industrial jumpsuits and sunglasses) and bizarre philosophy (the concept of 'de-evolution,' that mankind had begun to go backwards rather than evolving, witnessed by the dysfunction and consumerism of American society). The band released a couple of singles ("Mongoloid," "(I Can't Get No) Satisfaction") on its own independent Booji Boy label, bringing them to the attention of David Bowie and Iggy Pop, who helped the band get signed to Warner Brothers.

Bowie was evidently on the hook to produce Devo's debut, but previous commitments led to Brian Eno replacing him in the producer's chair for the creation of *Q: Are We Not Men? A: We Are Devo!* The band re-recorded its early singles (including the popular B-side "Jocko Homo") as well as a bunch of new originals like Mark Mothersbaugh's "Uncontrollable Urge," Gerald Casale's "Sloppy (I Saw My Baby Gettin')," and Mothersbaugh's "Too Much Paranoias."

The music was jumpy, dissonant, and edgy with odd time signatures and amateurish, tense vocals mixed with out-of-control guitar and synthesizer. The band's lyrics were satirical, humorously tongue-in-cheek, and intellectual – hardly the stuff of Top 40 prospects. Regardless of its odd duck status, *Are We Not Men* inched up to #78 on the *Billboard* album chart, the band striking gold two years later with its *Freedom of Choice* album and hit single "Whip It." The album advertising, feauturing a generic white male figure superimposed against a golf ball, satirized consumerism even while trying to sell listners on "the sound of things falling apart."

The Dictators' "Seach & Destroy" (1977)

An example of a rare major label ad for a band single, Asylum Records' graphics for the Dictators' cover of the Stooges' "Search and Destroy" are devastatingly exciting. With a shattered record literally exploding out of the *Manifest Destiny* album sleeve (the band's debut LP for Asylum), the album's title on the cover banner is replaced by the single's songs – "Search and Destroy" and band member Andy Shernoff's original "Sleepin' With The TV On" – and the record's status as the band's new single. An announcement of the Dictators' tour with U.K. punks the Stranglers anchors the advertisement. Everything from the subliminal use of the album's cover art to the type face used on the song's title at the top of the ad displays a kinetic energy not unlike the band's high-octane rock 'n' roll sound.

The Doors' *Morrison Hotel* (1970)

You'd think that with the Doors' fifth studio album in four years (plus 1970's live *Absolutely Free*, the less said about the better…), that Messrs. Morrison and company would begin to run out of musical ideas, but it wasn't so.

Whereas 1969's *The Soft Parade* witnessed a band treading water and wondering how to get out of the pool, just a year later *Morrison Hotel* found a re-energized, raw, and ready-to-rumble outfit revisiting their blues roots (the Texas-flavored "Roadhouse Blues" and "The Spy"); delving into psychedelic mysticism ("Indian Summer," "Waiting For The Sun"); and diving back into the existential deep end with the dark-hued, malevolent "Peace Frog."

Although *Morrison Hotel* yielded no hit singles (admittedly, "Peace Frog" grabbed a lot of FM airplay and "Roadhouse Blues" would rise as high as #50 on the singles chart), it was a commercially-successful mix of blues and hard rock (hitting #4 on the album chart) that paved the way for the blockbuster, career-making *L.A. Woman* album the following year.

Dwight Twilley Band's *Sincerely* (1976)

Although cult rocker Dwight Twilley scored a Top 20 hit single in the spring of 1975 with the infectious, melodic tune "I'm On Fire," he was nevertheless about five years too early for the 1980s power-pop revival he helped inspire and influence. For Twilley and musical partner Phil Seymour, it would take almost a year and a lot of false starts before they'd come up with a proper debut, 1976's excellent *Sincerely* album.

Sadly, it seemed to be a case of "too little, too late;" although *Sincerely* scratched its way onto the Top 200 chart (#138), there wouldn't be another "I'm On Fire" in the offing. The pair built upon a fine musical tradition that included similar cult faves as Crabby Appleton and Big Star, or even the moderately-successful Badfinger and the Raspberries, with songs like "Could Be Love," "Release Me," and "Baby Let's Cruise" finding an appreciative, albeit smallish audience.

The band's label, Leon Russell's Shelter Records, lacked the financial resources to fully promote *Sincerely*, but the advertising that accompanied the album masterfully evoked another time, a summertime of drive-in movies and intelligent pop-rock music of the Dwight Twilley Band variety.

Dwight Twilley Band's *Twilley Don't Mind* (1977)

Expectations were high for the Dwight Twilley Band after the critical acclaim afforded their debut album, *Sincerely*. The band's label, Shelter Records signed a deal with Arista Records to distribute their sophomore effort, and the material for *Twilley Don't Mind* was demoed well in advance of the recording sessions, so that the band – now featuring touring guitarist Bill Pitcock IV in a more prominent role – went into the studio with ten strong songs. The band had a difficult time getting "Fallin' In Love" to sound as they wanted, so *Twilley Don't Mind* was released with only nine tracks, "Fallin' In Love" not to appear again until it was used as a bonus track on a 1990 CD reissue. Labelmate Tom Petty, who was beginning to make some chart noise himself at the time, plays guitar on "Looking For The Magic."

The original cover artwork for *Twilley Don't Mind* was famously vetoed by Arista's autocratic leader, Clive Davis, who personally chose the album's replacement artwork. I have to agree with ol' Clive here, though, as the original cover art was pug ugly. The label's effective advertising campaign for the album used a photo from the session used for the final cover art, a glam shot of band members Dwight Twilley and Phil Seymour and the engaging tag line "Why you fell in love with rock 'n' roll in the first place" along with approving quotes about the album from *Crawdaddy* and *Phonograph Record* magazines. The ad's design and verbiage helped convince record buyers to check out the album.

While *Twilley Don't Mind* peaked at an encouraging #70 on the *Billboard* album chart, it proved to be the band's swansong as Seymour left a few months after the album's release to pursue a solo career, later briefly hooking up with roots-rockers the Textones. Sadly, Seymour was diagnosed with lymphoma in the mid-1980s and passed away in 1993; to this day, Twilley still won't perform Dwight Twilley Band songs that featured Seymour's lead vocals in honor of his late friend. As for Bill Pitcock IV, who was snubbed by the album's artwork and ad campaign, he continued to hang with his former band mates, playing lead guitar on Seymour's 1980 solo debut and on most of Twilley's solo albums to the present day.

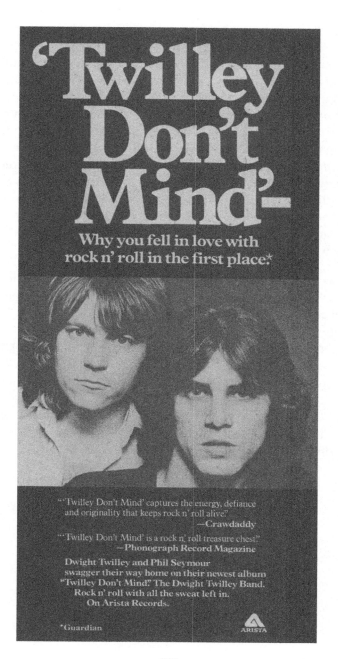

Bob Dylan's *Self Portrait* (1970)

Perhaps the most misunderstood and maligned of Dylan's early albums, and an inauspicious beginning to the decade of the 1970s (especially after the previous year's acclaimed, country-flavored *Nashville Skyline*), *Self Portrait* isn't quite the pail of lukewarm dishwater it's often made out to be. Confusing, yes, even to the sort of prawn that spends their lives trying to suss out the Shakespeare of Rock's every utterance. With *Self Portrait*, Dylan was literally providing us with a series of crudely-painted canvases, the singer often applying the broadest of strokes, but revealing glimpses of the face behind the cover with a mix of originals, outtakes, and cover songs that each displayed a facet of Dylan's temperament at the time…sometimes joking, sometimes playful (like a cat toying with a mouse), never less than thought-provoking.

Released as a two-album set with Dylan's original artwork gracing the cover, the two-dozen numbers on *Self Portrait* run the gamut from influential covers (Boudleaux Bryant's "Take Me As I Am" and "Take A Message To Mary"); contemporary cover songs (Paul Simon's "The Boxer," Gordon Lightfoot's "Early Morning Rain"); vintage folk tunes ("Days of '49"); and old material, including outtakes from *The Basement Tapes* sessions ("The Mighty Quinn," "Like A Rolling Stone"). Taken altogether, critics at the time considered it a rambling mess unworthy of an artist of Dylan's stature. I prefer to think of it as a psychic "cleaning out of the closet" that would lead to the undisputedly brilliant *New Morning* album. Still, *Self Portrait* has its adherents, as shown by Sony's decision to release an expanded "deluxe" reissue version of the album in late 2013.

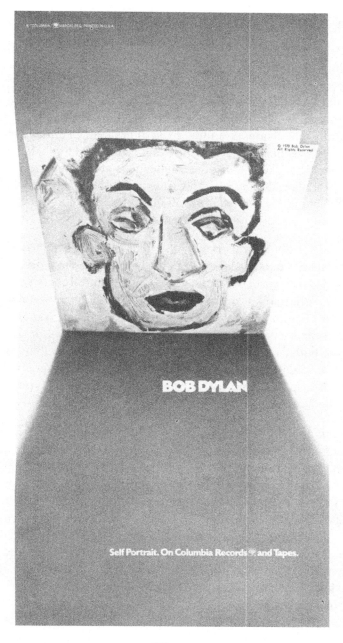

Brian Eno's *Before and After Science* (1977)

Brian Peter George St. John le Baptiste de la Salle Eno made his bones as a utility player with Roxy Music during the band's early '70s "glam rock" period, adding keyboards, synthesizers, and cutting edge tape manipulation to Roxy's unique sound. Clad in make-up and feathered boas, Eno often "out glammed" glamorous Roxy frontman Bryan Ferry, and the musical visionary left the band after a pair of albums to pursue a restless and wandering artistic muse that has earned him a legacy as one of rock music's greatest all-time intellectuals and visionaries. A 1973 musical collaboration with King Crimson's Robert Fripp resulted in the groundbreaking *No Pussyfooting* album, the pair following up the effort in 1975 with the equally-audacious *Evening Star*.

As a producer, Eno has worked with artists like U2, David Bowie, and Talking Heads, and he's lent his talents in the studio to a diverse crop of like-minded artists such as John Cale, Cluster, and Robert Wyatt. Eno's own solo work remains a stellar representation of his musical and artistic obsessions, beginning with the hard-rocking 1973 disc *Here Come The Warm Jets* and the following year's *Taking Tiger Mountain (By Strategy)*, both extremely influential albums. His 1975 album *Another Green World* began Eno's artistic evolution towards minimalist, Krautrock-inspired "ambient" music, largely eschewing lyrics in favor of aural soundscapes.

Before and After Science, released in 1977, continued Eno's quest into the avant garde, the album composed entirely in the studio by recording and layering instrumentation, selectively subtracting from the tracks until Eno achieved the sound he was seeking. The label's ad for the album is a minimalist delight, constructed with multiple copies of the LP cover and Eno clones standing with arms folded above the fray. Quotes from such rockcrit stalwarts as Lester Bangs and John Rockwell finished the tableau, which didn't really need much more. Eno fans may not have known exactly *what* they were going to hear from the artist by this point, but we knew what they *weren't* going to hear and, for many of us, that was enough...

The Fabulous Poodles' *Mirror Stars* (1978)

Were they pub rockers or new wave jokers? A little from column 'A' and a little from column 'B,' perhaps; formed in 1975 and breaking up in 1980, Britain's the Fabulous Poodles straddled both musical genres effortlessly. Heavily influenced by '60s-era British Invasion bands like the Who and the Kinks, the Poodles incorporated the melodic sense and three-chord dynamics of the '60s in creating their cheeky "new wave" soundtrack. The band released three albums during their brief tenure – their 1977 self-titled debut, produced by the Who's John Entwistle; 1978's *Unsuitable*, produced by the Spencer Davis Group's Muff Winwood; and a third and final effort, 1979's classic *Think Pink*.

The Poodles failed to achieve a commercial breakthrough on either side of the pond, but they made quite a splash nevertheless. Legendary British DJ John Peel cited them as his favorite band at the time, and they toured with the likes of Meat Loaf, Tom Petty & the Heartbreakers, and the Ramones, and even backed the great Chuck Berry on a U.K. tour. Neither of the band's first two albums were released stateside, a heinous crime in my eyes, and were available only as costly import platters.

Mirror Stars, released in 1978, was a compilation LP, picking and choosing about half the songs from the band's first two English albums for U.S. audiences. *Mirror Stars* featured some of the Poodles' best work, including the title track and songs like "Work Shy," "Mr. Mike," "B Movies," and "Chicago Boxcar (Boston Back)," a minor U.K. hit. But there was also a lot of meat left on the bone, and it would have cost little or nothing to reissue both Poodles LPs for a domestic audience.

Still, American fans had to make do with only half of the band's recordings, and the ad campaign for *Mirror Stars* provided the Poodles no favors. A clever cut 'n' fold construct with pictures of the album cover and the band is OK, but the ad copy is pure-grade gibberish from some word-junkie lurking in the shadows of Epic Records' 52nd street basement. Bad puns aside, the ad did little to sell the album but then, with little on the line financially, the label didn't have to care one way or another…

THE FABULOUS POODLES
MIRROR STARS
including:
Mirror Star/Work Shy/B Movies
Chicago Boxcar/Toytown People

THE FABULOUS POODLES DOO IT HERE.

Instructions

Carefully fold, spindle and mutilate this piece of foolscap for your very own doggie device (suitable for scooping), courtesy of Britain's fashionably anthropomorphic Fabulous Poodles.

"Right now, the Poodles must be the tackiest band in the country," avers England's Sounds.

So proceed at a brisk trot to the Fab Poos' recorded boner, the deluxe new album "Mirror Stars."

Lovingly produced by John Entwistle and Muff Winwood in the great Anglo art-school tradition, the Fabulous Poodles win, place and show their satiric fangs and ferocious instrumental chops with a litter full of irresistibly shaggy songs.

"The Poodles combine mature musicianship with gross juvenile humor," adduces the New Musical Express.

"We're Poodles, not punks," avow the quatre canines.

Listen for yourself and find out why Poodles make such Fabulous house pets.

Even though they bite the hands that feed them. "Mirror Stars." A substantial doggie dinner from the Fabulous Poodles. On Epic Records and Tapes.

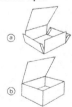

(a)

(b)

CUT ALONG LINE

Faces' *Ooh La La* (1973)

In the three years following the Faces' rise, phoenix-like, from the ashes of British mod-era rockers the Small Faces, it had been a hell of a party. Although albums like 1971's *Long Player* and *A Nod Is as Good As a Wink...to a Blind Horse* are now considered rock 'n' roll classics, and both were modest-to-impressive commercial successes (the former hitting #29 on the charts, the latter rising to #6 on the strength of the hit single "Stay With Me"), by the time of 1973's *Ooh La La*, frontman Rod Stewart's solo success had begun to outshine his erstwhile band. *Ooh La La* would take a step backwards on the charts, rising only as far as #21 and yielding no hit singles; by contrast, Stewart's fourth solo album, the previous year's *Never A Dull Moment*, hit #2 on the charts and coughed up a pair of hits.

While it was apparent to anybody at the time that Stewart was sliding, albeit in slow-motion, towards the door on his way to exiting for a full-time solo jaunt, that doesn't mean that *Ooh La La* doesn't have its charms. Rod the Mod may have been gracing magazine covers instead of, say, bandmates Ron Wood or Ian McLagen, but *Ooh La La* was a true group effort, with all five members involved in the songwriting, resulting in great tunes like "Cindy Incidentally" and "Borstal Boys." It was bassist Ronnie Lane, one of the original Small Faces, who was the band's creative heart, and he dominated the songwriting on the album's second half, providing the Faces with a fitting swansong for their final album.

The Warner Brothers label ad for the album was a perfect portrayal of the band's public image, the reckless rockers gazing upwards at the upturned skirt of the dancing girl as the album cover's leering visage sits in the top right corner. When the label called *Ooh La La* the Faces' "sauciest album," they may have been partly kidding, but they also weren't that far off the mark!

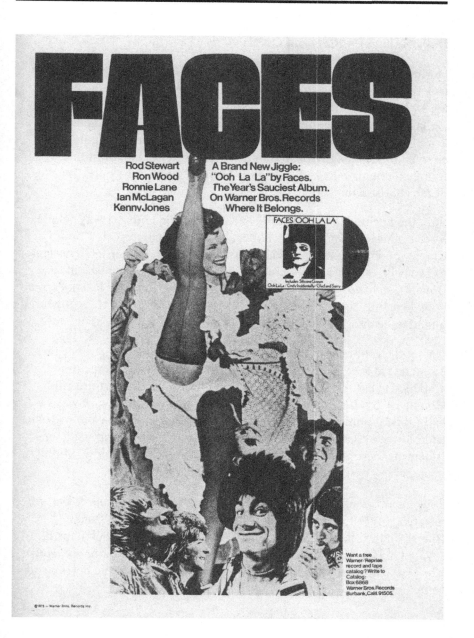

Rory Gallager's *Blueprint* (1973)

During a career that ranged from his late 1960s albums with the power trio Taste to a prolific solo career that remained vital from the release of his 1971 debut until his death in 1995, blues-rock guitarist Rory Gallagher earned a status as rock 'n' roll's everyman. Gallagher never achieved much commercial success through the years – although he enjoyed modest chart position in the U.K., fewer than half of the fourteen albums released during his lifetime scraped the upper reaches of the charts in the U.S.

Still, the talented, hard drinking, and charismatic guitarist was beloved by fans and fellow musicians alike, and artists as diverse as Eric Clapton, U2's The Edge, Vivian Campbell of Def Leppard, Glenn Tipton of Judas Priest, Slash from Guns N' Roses, and blues wunderkind Joe Bonamassa have cited Gallagher as an influence. It might be apocryphal, but when Jimi Hendrix was asked how it felt to be the world's greatest guitarist, he allegedly stated "I don't know, go ask Rory Gallagher."

One of the problems that consistently plagued Gallagher's career is that his stateside label, Polydor Records, had no idea how to hype his albums. Take this pug ugly advertisement for Gallagher's third studio album, 1973's *Blueprint*. Although the album's cover artwork wasn't bad, some graphic designer decided to strip the LP art down to its basics and blow it up large with the absurd "This is a copy of Rory Gallagher's Blueprint" across the top and "The original is for sale" below. Mighty inane, in my opinion…what would have been better?

How about some sort of reference to Gallagher's blues roots as part of his creative 'blueprint' (he did cover Big Bill Broonzy's "Banker's Blues" on the album)? No matter…with red-hot blooze-rock jams like "Walk On Hot Coals" and "Seventh Son of the Seventh Son," *Blueprint* was Gallagher's first album to chart stateside in spite of the horrible ad campaign on his behalf…

Gentle Giant's *Octopus* (1972)

By 1972, British rockers Gentle Giant were firmly entrenched in the mid-tier of progressive rock outfits, a step behind more successful chartbusters like Yes and Emerson, Lake & Palmer and not as highly regarded as critical darlings like King Crimson and Jethro Tull. Instead, they were kind of lumped in together with bands like Starcastle and the Strawbs, esteemed groups that enjoyed pockets of fandom but achieving only a modicum of commercial success. Although Gentle Giant would eventually transcend its cult band status to be considered one of the important and influential movers and shakers of 1970s-era prog-rock, with the release of their fourth album *Octopus*, they were just looking for a hit.

Although *Octopus* received uniformly positive reviews, with rockcrit handicappers predicting it to be the band's breakthrough moment, Columbia Records' advertising for the album did little to support Gentle Giant's chart aspirations. Lauded for the virtuoso musicianship displayed by band founders the Shulman brothers (Derek, Phil & Ray), as well as guitarist Gary Green and drummer/multi-instrumentalist Kerry Minnear, *Octopus* sported an intriguing John Berg cover design that portrayed a stylized cephalopod captured in a jar. Columbia's ad featured Berg's striking cover front and center and larger than life, tagging it with a horrible pun ("a jarring new album"…really, what were you guys smoking/snorting to come up with a line like that?) and reducing the descriptive text to the fine print at the bottom of the page.

They'd have been better off reducing the size of the dominating graphic (which is reproduced again at the bottom of the ad) and including short, pithy, easy-to-read descriptions of the band and the album instead of the dense text that nobody bothered to dig through. By this time, the band's fan base was pretty much set in stone, and *Octopus* only rose to #170 on the *Billboard* Top 200 before sinking. Although Gentle Giant would call it quits in 1980, they still had a couple of masterpieces up their sleeve and *Octopus*, along with the following year's *In A Glass House* and 1975's *Free Hand*, would prove to be the cornerstones of the band's enduring legacy.

ANNOUNCING A JARRING NEW ALBUM FROM GENTLE GIANT.

Gentle Giant's latest effort, "Octopus," is a fine specimen. It jumps from texture to texture and rhythm to rhythm with all the exuberance and eclecticism G.G. fans have come to expect. One minute they might be into driving instrumental rock, when suddenly they'll do a complex a *cappella* vocal part that sounds like a jam between Don Carlo Gesualdo and the Harptones.

The six members of the group can play literally dozens of instruments. In fact, on stage they switch instruments so freely, it's hard to keep track of who's playing what.

Some G.G. addicts got hooked on imports of their first two British-only albums; others on their Columbia debut, "Three Friends." Still others became believers when they caught Gentle Giant live on one of their American tours. Now (hopefully) it's time for you to take the plunge with "Octopus," the latest album by Gentle Giant.

On Columbia Records ✸

GENTLE GIANT
Octopus
including:
Knots/The Advent Of Panurge
Raconteur Troubadour/The Boys In The Band
Dog's Life

Also available on tape

Jimi Hendrix's *High, Live'n Dirty* **(1978)**

National Lampoon in the '70s was the comedy zine of choice for the suburban teen intelligentsia. Ostensibly aimed towards an older, more sophisticated audience, the *Lampoon* kept us chuckling during our high school daze with scatological humor, gratuitous nudity, and absurdist satire that whetted our appetite for musical equivalents like Firesign Theatre and the Bonzo Dog Band. Although advertising in the magazine was aimed at adults with lifestyle consumer products like turntables and stereo systems, the publication also ran the occasional album advertising, like this piece for the questionable Jimi Hendrix LP *High, Live'n Dirty*.

A dodgy, unauthorized release by some fly-by-night label, Hendrix's *High, Live'n Dirty* is a bit of a conundrum to aficionados and amateur musical sleuths alike. Some have said that it's an early vinyl version of the infamous Hendrix bootleg *Woke Up This Morning And Found Myself Dead*, itself released in 1980. Allegedly capturing a late night 'jam' between Jimi and bluesman Johnny Winter at NYC club The Scene in 1968, with obscene spoken word vocals by Jim Morrison dubbed in (he doesn't seem to have been at the club that night), the tracklist for *High, Live'n Dirty* doesn't match up with its doppelganger, further enhancing the mystery.

The album was released on vibrant red vinyl, and the Nutmeg Records' ad must have been effective, because copies of the album seem easy to find (implying a lot of original purchases), currently selling for less than $20 on eBay.

Iggy and the Stooges' *Raw Power* (1973)

The early 1970s was a tumultuous time for Iggy Pop and the (Psychedelic) Stooges. While the band had released a pair of critically-acclaimed albums in *The Stooges* (1969) and *Fun House* (1970) that would eventually become influential icons of rock music, both albums were deemed commercial busts and the band couldn't get arrested even in their Motor City hometown. As the various members drifted into hardcore substance abuse, Iggy tried to keep the band afloat by juggling the line-up and adding underrated guitarist James Williamson, but it looked as if the Stooges were about to become footnotes in rock 'n' roll history when an unexpected savior stepped in to put the band on the road to immortality.

A chance meeting in 1972 between Iggy Pop and David Bowie would lead to the British glam-rock star taking the wheel of the badly listing Stooges ship of state and, temporarily at least, setting the band on a straight course. Bowie's manager took on the band, and the singer – who was at the height of his *Ziggy Stardust* era fame – took the band into the studio to record their important, influential third album. Released in 1973, *Raw Power* would ultimately provide a template for young punks around the world to follow just a couple years later, and songs like "Search and Destroy," "Gimme Danger," "Your Pretty Face Is Going To Hell," and the high-octane title track would inspire several subsequent generations of young, loud, and snotty rockers.

The Columbia Records ad for the album featured the iconic photo of a young Iggy Stooge strangling the microphone alongside influential quotes from *Creem*'s Dave Marsh and *Rolling Stone*'s Lenny Kaye (future Patti Smith Band guitarist)...simple, but effective, conveying both the band's sense of danger (now billed as "Iggy and the Stooges") and the energetic nature of the music in the grooves.

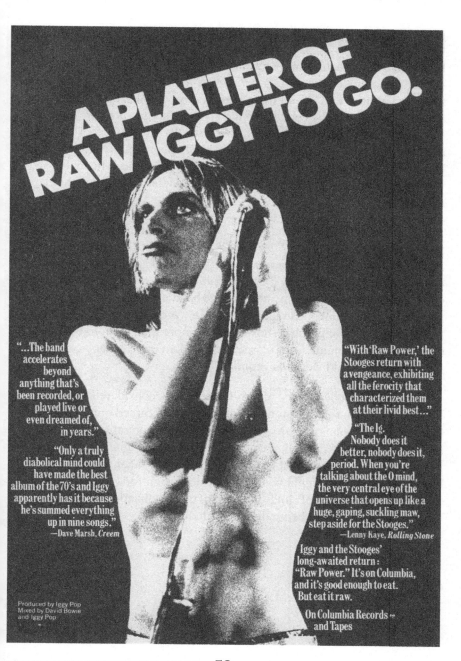

Jefferson Airplane's *Volunteers* (1972)

Released during the dimming days of the "peace & love" decade of the 1960s, the Jefferson Airplane's *Volunteers* was, arguably, both one of their best albums and one of their most controversial. The band's leftist, anti-war politics shone brightly in the lyrics of songs like "We Can Be Together" (in which the label tried to censor the word "motherfucker") and the title track while songs like "Good Shepherd" and "Eskimo Blue Day" evinced more of a "back to the land," hippie vibe. Musically, *Volunteers* ranged from hippie folk and psychdelia to anthemic hard rock.

The album extended the band's string of five straight Top 20 albums, peaking at #13 on the *Billboard* Top 200 while the title track rose to #65, quite an accomplishment for a politically-charged song at the dawn of the AOR era. The label's ad for the album certainly didn't help its commercial prospects – I'm sure that the band's high-profile performance at the Woodstock festival a few months previous did more for *Volunteers* – the graphic showing little more than a photo of the LP cover, the band's name in too-large type, and an out-of-place copy of Dan O'Neill's "Odd Bodkins" comic.

Volunteers would be the last album from what is considered to be the band's classic line-up, drummer Spencer Dryden forced out and replaced by Joey Covington, singer Marty Balin to follow soon thereafter, before the 1971 release of *Bark*, the band's sixth Top 20 LP in a row and the first for its RCA-distributed Grunt Records vanity label. Considering how little effort or thought went into the ad design for *Volunteers*, or even the album cover of *Bark*, one wonders if the band was too stoned to realized that they were being dissed by the label.

Jefferson Starship's *Spitfire* (1976)

What a difference a few years makes – discarding Jefferson Airplane frontman Paul Kanter's solo debut *Blows Against The Empire*, which was credited to Kanter and "Jefferson Starship" and was more of a hard rock hippie fever dream – by 1974, the Airplane had been grounded, the band adding new guitarist Craig Chaquico and bassist Pete Sears (to replace band founders Jorma Kaukonen and Jack Casady, who had gone full-time with their Hot Tuna side project) and taking flight anew as Jefferson Starship. The 1974 release of the Starship's *Dragon Fly* would hit #11 on the charts, but the following year's *Red Octopus* would rise to #1 on the strength of the #3 hit single "Miracles."

The Starship's third album as a full band, 1976's *Spitfire*, couldn't boast of material the strength of "Miracles," but it rode high on the charts nonetheless, sitting at #3 for three weeks and eventually selling better than a million copies. The album's colorful cover artwork was certainly striking, the brilliant graphics making for a memorable ad that featured an enigmatic female figure astride an Asian styled dragon and, at the bottom, the album's name. Although the label stepped up its game for the album art, the ad itself is pretty lazy, saying nothing about the band or music and relying instead on the LP imagery itself to sell the product.

Jo Jo Gunne's *Bite Down Hard* (1973)

Boogie rockers Jo Jo Gunne were formed in 1971 by former Spirit members Jay Ferguson (vocals) and Mark Andes (bass), with Mark's brother Matt (guitar) and Curly Smith (drums) rounding out the line-up. The band's self-titled 1972 debut scored a Top 30 U.S. hit with the single "Run Run Run" (Top 10 in the U.K.), the album itself hitting a respectable #57 on the U.S. charts. Mark Andes fell out with his brother and Ferguson after the debut album's release and left the band for a stint with Firefall before hooking up with Heart for an extended run.

Undaunted, Jo Jo Gunne brought in new bassist Jimmie Randall, who would stay with the band through its bloody end, and they rushed into the studio to record a follow-up to their debut in order to capitalize on its relative success. *Bite Down Hard* was the result, a similarly boogie-based high-octane set that nevertheless sounds rushed, tired, and repetitive. There was too much of the same raucous vibe that fueled the debut, but no single song popped and crackled like "Run Run Run" and, lacking an obvious hit single, the album struggled to hit #75 on the charts.

Asylum Records certainly supplied an eye-catching advertisement to push the new album, even if it did little to improve the band's diminishing fortunes. Featuring a pair of cartoon teeth chomping down on a bullet and the tagline "music you can really get your teeth into," it's an irreverent attempt to introduce rock fans to *Bite Down Hard* while making a cheeky play on the album's title.

The band's third album in two years, *Jumpin' The Gunne*, was essentially a Jay Ferguson solo album and would be saddled with atrocious cover artwork that did nothing to help it barely squirm its way onto the charts (peaking at #169). Matt Andes left after this third album, to be replaced by John Staehley, another Spirit alumnus. One more disc would emerge – 1974's *So...Where's The Show* – which would be the band's hardest rocking and consistent album. It was a case of too little, too late, as Jo Jo Gunne burned out from too much touring, too many records, and only one hit to show for their work.

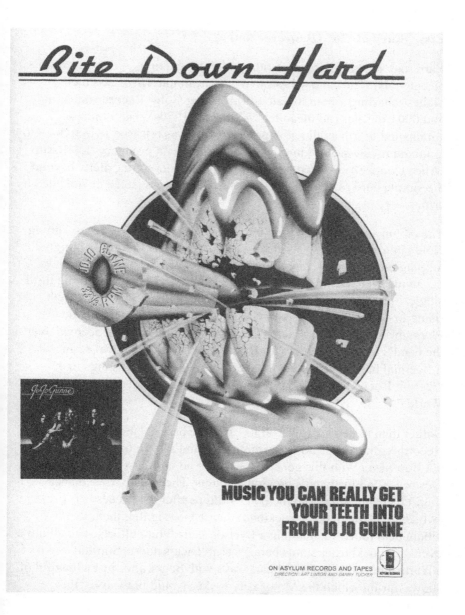

Kiss "Spirit of '76" (*Destroyer* tour)

Hard rock legends Kiss were riding high by the time of the American bicentennial. The band's 1975 live double album *Alive!* was their highest-charting album to date (#9), earning Gold® Record status for 500,000+ in sales (no mean feat in the mid-1970s). Their much-anticipated fourth studio album, *Destroyer*, was released in March 1976 to mixed reviews. Working for the first time with producer Bob Ezrin (Alice Cooper, Lou Reed), the band expanded its sonic palette beyond the simple hard rock of its earlier efforts, a move rejected or ridiculed by critics.

The album sold rapidly on the basis of its predecessor's success, going Gold® in a month and peaking at #11 on the charts before seemingly topping out at slightly more than 800,000 copies sold. When deejays began playing "Beth," the B-side of the album's underperforming third single, "Detroit Rock City," it reignited the album's fortunes, "Beth" rising to #7 on the singles chart and pushing the album to double Platinum™ sales. The album's initial stumble would be redeemed over the band's lengthy career, with Destroyer becoming known as an influential hard rock/heavy metal effort on the basis of songs like "Detroit Rock City," "Shout It Out Loud," and "King of the Night Time World."

Rather than hype *Destroyer* on its own, the band's label – Casablanca Records – chose instead to promote the band's 1976 tour with opening act Bob Seger with this generic tour dates ad with just a passing nod to *Destroyer* and the band's previous albums. Then again, Casablanca didn't have much faith in the band's future after the success of *Alive!* (which made the label a truckload of cash), re-signing them to a two-album deal rather than taking a flyer on their future efforts. The album's eventual blockbuster status belies Casablanca's non-committal advertising, and Kiss would part ways with Seger after just a handful of shows during which the Motor City rocker would blow away the headliners night after night.

Kraftwerk's *Radio-Activity* (1975)

German electronic music pioneers Kraftwerk enjoyed an unexpected level of success when the band's fourth album, 1974's *Autobahn*, scored a surprising Top 30 chart hit with its title track. The popularity of "Autobahn," cut down from the album length of 22+ minutes to a mere 3:27 for radio airplay, pushed the album itself to number five on the *Billboard* chart. It would be the band's lone U.S. hit, and although they would continue to make music well into the 1980s, they'd never again achieve this level of commercial success stateside.

The band's modest achievement didn't go to their collective heads, as shown by the 1975 release of Kraftwerk's *Radio-Activity* album. A return to the more electronically-oriented noisemaking of their earlier work, the album's conceptual aesthetic – exploring the subject of radio waves and outer space – was bolstered by scraps of bleeping sound, silent passages, raucous noise, and overall electronic weirdness. The album's lone concession to commercial reality came in the form of Kraftwerk's first English language song in the title track. While garnering critical accolades, the album's lone single (the title track) stiffed badly, and *Radio-Activity* only rose as high as #140 on the charts.

Capitol Records really had no idea what to do with Kraftwerk or *Radio-Activity*, but the simple B&W ad created for the album was oddly effective. Utilizing the simple black box from the album cover, they tacked on a photo of the band in a frame on top. For Krautrock fans, this was more than enough as the announcement of a new Kraftwerk LP was cause for rejoice in certain circles.

The band would find a modicum of success with subsequent albums like *Trans-Europe Express* (1977) and *Computer World* (1981), especially when their electronic tunes were adapted to 1980s dance culture. Kraftwerk's influence would be wide-ranging, their musical innovations touching such disparate genres as hip-hop, EDM, keyboards-dominated new wave, and avant-garde composition.

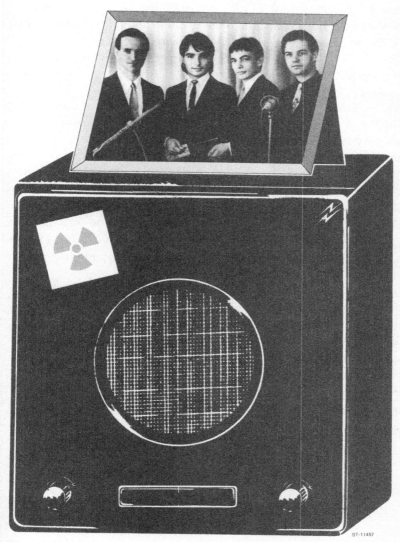

ST-11457

Capitol

Led Zeppelin's *Houses of the Holy* (1973)

Sitting on top of the world in 1973, Jimmy Page and his fellow gang members in Led Zeppelin felt little need to follow the rules of polite society. When the label pressured them to come up with a name for their untitled fourth album, Page provided them with a set of cryptic runes. The album sold millions of flapjacks in spite of its anonymity, as fans figured it out anyway. Zep's fifth album, *Houses of the Holy*, was its first in four years to not receive a numbered title.

The album was not without its own controversy, however – the imaginative cover art, created by Aubrey Powell of Hipgnosis, features a number of apparently naked children crawling across the stones of some ancient, arcane temple. Some retailers, especially in the Southern U.S. states, refused to stock the album because of its cover (relax, people – the kids were wearing body suits). Like its predecessor, neither the album's title nor the band name adorned the cover of *Houses of the Holy*, although a paper wrapper with the info was strategically-strapped around the cover to block out the horribly naked (and oddly colored) children.

Also like Led Zeppelin's fourth effort, fans promptly figured out the ruse, and *Houses of the Holy* would eventually move better than ten million copies worldwide, topping the charts in the United States, Canada, Australia, and the U.K. The print advertising for *Houses of the Holy* eschewed the album's brilliant cover artwork in favor of cool Victorian-era styled B&W pen-and-ink art that showed a bound man's head being squeezed in a viselike contraption between two railway cars. A simple tagline beneath the album's title read "does things to people..." For Zep's legion of rabid, cash-toting fans, nothing else needed to be said...

MC5's *Back In The USA* (1970)

Detroit's favorite sonic terrorists, the infamous MC5, were an oddity even in the late 1960s. The band's first album, 1969's *Kick Out The Jams*, was recorded live at Russ Gibbs' legendary Grande Ballroom venue, capturing the dynamic band onstage and raging against the machine. As such, *Back In The USA*, the band's sophomore effort, was actually their studio debut. Even in those days, a band usually had a couple of studio records under their belt before shooting for a live disc.

But MC5 were no ordinary band, and their deep repertoire of original material and inspired covers of blues, soul, and jazz sides allowed them to introduce themselves with a high-octane live collection that would hit #30 on the charts on the strength of its incendiary title track. *Back In The USA* was a different kind of beast, however – produced by rock critic Jon Landau (who would later become Bruce Springsteen's manager), the album masterfully blended punkish intensity with a raucous, melodic power-pop sound that would yield some of the band's best original songs in "Teenage Lust," "High School," and "Shakin' Street," songs that would in turn influence bands like the Dictators, the Flamin' Groovies, and the New York Dolls, among others.

Atlantic's ad campaign for *Back In The USA* was simple – a black and white photo of the band, clad in leather jackets with a collective sneer on their faces, looking like a gang of ruffians (an image later appropriated to good use by the Ramones). Beneath the dominant band photo is a list of the album's songs, and a shot of the cover. Although *Back In The USA* found nowhere near the success of its predecessor, rising only as high as #137 on the charts, its influence would cross the decades. It has since become considered a high water mark for the legendary band, and you can hear strains of MC5 in the music of the White Stripes, the Clash, the Dead Kennedys, Radio Birdman, and other bands across the spectrum of the rock, punk, and metal genres.

BACK IN THE USA

THE MC5

Includes: Tutti-Frutti • Tonight • Teenage Lust • Let Me Try • Looking At You • High School • Call Me Animal • The American Ruse • Shakin' Street • The Human Being Lawnmower • Back In The USA

On Atlantic Records & Tapes

Felix Pappalardi's *Felix Pappalardi & Creation* (1976)

It could easily be argued that musician, songwriter, and producer Felix Pappalardi was one of the architects of hard rock and heavy metal music. Although he originally honed his production chops working on folk and folk-rock records by artists like Tim Hardin, the Youngbloods, and Joan Baez, among others, he hooked up with Eric Clapton and Cream for their second album, producing *Disraeli Gears* and later becoming known as the band's fourth member. He went on to produce Cream's *Wheels of Fire* (1968) and *Goodbye* (1969) albums, as well as Cream bassist Jack Bruce's 1969 solo debut, *Songs For A Tailor*.

Pappalardi, a classically-trained musician, would become best-known for his role as bass player and producer of one of the heaviest dinosaur-rock outfits that would stomp across the planet in Mountain. Pappalardi had previously worked in the studio with guitarist Leslie West's band the Vagrants, and when Cream broke up, ol' Felix saw an opportunity for a like-minded power trio. Enlisting the larger-than-life guitarist and vocalist to front Mountain, the band's first two albums would go Gold™ in the U.S. and result in a classic rock radio staple in the song "Mississippi Queen." When Mountain broke-up, Pappalardi semi-retired from touring due to rock 'n' roll-induced partial deafness; he later returned to the studio to produce records by the Flock, Hot Tuna, and even punk rock legends the Dead Boys.

In 1976, Pappalardi hooked up with Japanese hard rockers Creation, who had opened for Mountain during the band's earlier tour of Japan, for a one-off record titled *Felix Pappalardi & Creation*. They benefited from a high-profile tour, opening for Bob Seger and Kiss, but lacking the charismatic presence of the larger-than-life West, the album went nowhere fast. The label's ad for Felix Pappalardi & Creation was certainly grand enough, the bass player standing front and center with a rising sun behind him, his head haloed by rays of light. It plays up his impressive bona fides, but it may have been too little, too late. Pappalardi would make his proper solo debut with 1979's *Don't Worry, Ma* collection of covers. Tragically, a Mountain reunion would occur without the accomplished bassist, as Pappalardi was shot to death in 1983 by his songwriter wife Gail Collins.

Polydor Records' "Rock 'N' Rule Britania" ad (1979)

Grouping all of a company's hot new releases in a single magazine ad was a tried-and-true technique for getting the most bang for your marketing dollar for major record labels in the '70s. This Polydor Records' advertisement celebrating the 5th anniversary of *Trouser Press* music zine in 1979, provided the label the best of both worlds – all the benefits of supporting an important milestone of a worthwhile publication while still managing to hype your current crop of transformative rock 'n' roll vinyl.

Looking at this Polydor ad in retrospect, the six albums featured provide an amazing glimpse into the diverse and creative artists slaving away on the corporate plantation for the British label. I tackle the ad that accompanied the release of 10cc's *Bloody Tourists* further on in the book, but aside from Pat Travers' modestly-successful *Heat In The Street* LP, there were no real smash hits hyped by the ad, just the kind of free-wheeling and adventuresome rock music that *Trouser Press* was known to promote.

The Jam's *All Mod Cons* album has since become known as a classic of British rock while 10cc refugees Lol Crème and Kevin Godley's art-rock album *L* would have been a shaky release for any label. British folk-rock heroes Barclay James Harvest had been kicking around the isle for a few years by this point without ever breaking through in the U.S. Guitar god Travers was still rockin' hockey barns and stadiums at this point, and former Roxy Music fretburner Phil Manzanera's *K-Scope* album was influential albeit with limited commercial potential. Altogether, Polydor threw the dice and advertised a (mostly) risky group of new releases that were nevertheless pitch-perfect for the *Trouser Press* readership.

Ralph Records' "Musick For Weirdos" ad (1978)

Not so much an advertisement for a single album release but rather a clever slab o' bloato-hype from avant-garde indie label Ralph Records for a slew of their releases. Formed in 1972 in San Francisco by cult rockers the Residents when they realized that no corporate label would come anywhere near the band without a hazmat suit and ten-foot-pole, Ralph's first album release came in 1974 with the extraordinary *Meet The Residents*, as bizarre-o a chunk of PVC as one would ever slap on a turntable. After their acclaimed debut, Residents' albums fell like acid rain on the outer fringes of American rock 'n' roll, beginning with 1976's *The Third Reich 'n Roll* and following with 1977's *Fingerprince*, 1978's *Not Available* and the oddball *Duck Stab!/Buster & Glen*, a compilation of the band's seven-song *Duck Stab!* EP on the A-side and *Buster & Glen* holding down the B-side of the album.

The Residents evidently attracted a lot of like-minded fellow-travelers, and Ralph Records began releasing 45rpm singles and full-length albums by a number of, ah…shall we say 'unique' artists who fell into orbit around the label. The first was guitarist Philip "Snakefinger" Lithman, whose 7" single "The Spot" was release by Ralph in 1978, followed by a wonderful full-length album the next year, *Chewing Hides The Sound* featuring songwriting and musical contributions by the Residents as well as covers of Kraftwerk's "The Model" and composer Ennio Morricone's "Magic and Ecstasy," from the soundtrack of the movie *Exorcist II: The Heretic*. Of Snakefinger's debut LP, the *All Music Guide*'s Tom Schulte says "this is the peculiar and unique material of a cult guitarist extraordinaire. Each song is a quirky island in a sea of sonic oddity."

Snakefinger would record five albums total for Ralph Records, as well as a number of singles and appearances on several of the Residents' albums. The label would go on to release and promote music from a number of original, singular artists during the 1980s and '90s, including Fred Frith, Voice Farm, Tuxedomoon, MX-80 Sound, Renaldo and the Loaf, and the 'King' of the American underground, Eugene Chadbourne. This advertisement, culled from an old issue of *Trouser Press* – perhaps the only music zine to pay attention to Ralph Records and its bastard children – is a striking and effective way to promote the label's releases, displaying cover shots of several singles/EPs along with the label's recognizable logo. An almost subliminal phrase "you will buy lots of Ralph Records" is repeated in the background, and the label's address on the side encourages the curious to send off for a catalog…an important bit of marketing that seems quaint in the Internet era…

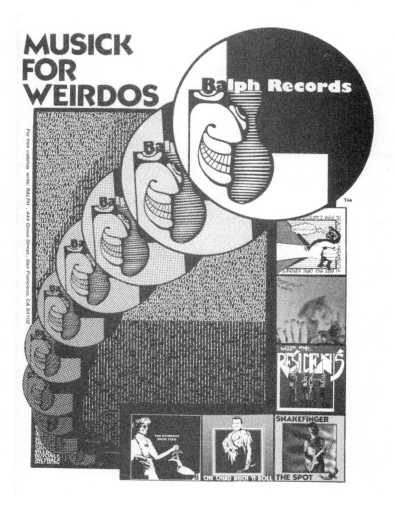

The Residents' *Eskimo* (1979)

The anonymous, oddball Residents were no less enigmatic on *Eskimo*, their sixth album, than they were with their curious 1974 debut, *Meet The Residents*. Releasing six albums in five years is extremely difficult for the most ambitious of bands, but the Residents faced the challenge head-on with the challenging suite of songs that comprised *Eskimo*. Ostensibly a concept album based on Eskimo culture (and music?), *Eskimo* the album is less a sojourn into ethnomusicology than it was a breathtaking hybrid of avant-garde sonics, ambient music, tribal rhythms, and electronic experimentation that would put the band at the forefront of a musical revolution entirely of their own making (but would later influence bands like the Talking Heads and Pere Ubu).

Since the Residents released all their early albums through their own Ralph Records imprint, they had total control over advertising artwork and venue (Ralph label ads frequently ran in Ira Robbins' forward-thinking *Trouser Press* music zine). The ad artwork for *Eskimo* is as stark and stunningly noticeable as any previous Ralph Records ad, jutting black lines approximating the unforgiving landscape preserved by the album's cover, with a bit of text that pseudo-seriously describes the album's concept; of course, the ever-present catalog pitch urged the reader to write away for a free Ralph Records catalog. If a music lover was even remotely interested in trying 'something different,' the Residents always delivered the goods.

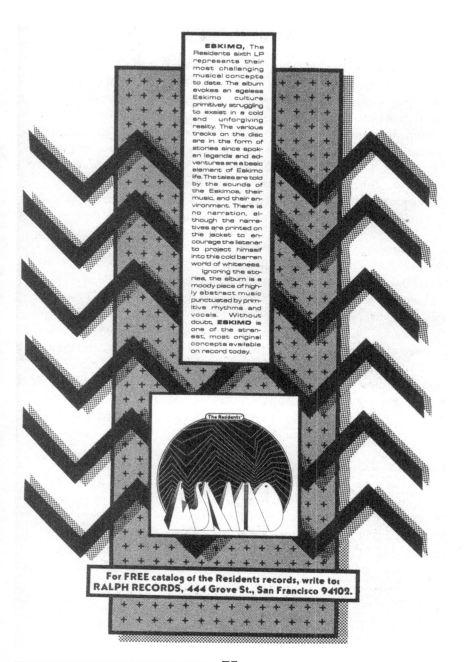

ESKIMO, The Residents sixth LP represents their most challenging musical concepts to date. The album evokes an ageless Eskimo culture primitively struggling to exsist in a cold and unforgiving reality. The various tracks on the disc are in the form of stories since spoken legends and adventures are a basic element of Eskimo life. The tales are told by the sounds of the Eskimos, their music, and their environment. There is no narration, although the narratives are printed on the jacket to encourage the listener to project himself into this cold barren world of whiteness.

Ignoring the stories, the album is a moody piece of highly abstract music punctuated by primitive rhythms and vocals. Without doubt, **ESKIMO** is one of the strangest, most original concepts available on record today.

The Residents'

For FREE catalog of the Residents records, write to:
RALPH RECORDS, 444 Grove St., San Francisco 94102.

Roxy Music's *For Your Pleasure* (1973)

Ah, the joys of '70s-era "glam rock"…the sugary icing atop the tasty cake that was hard rock during the era. Glam rock brought music lovers such ephemeral artists as Gary Glitter, Jobriath, Alvin Stardust, and Cockney Rebel. Second only to the following decade's 'New Romantic' movement, glam rock was ultimately disposable and designed from the ground up to eat up the charts and separate gullible tweens from their allowances. That's not to say that bands of the era were without talent or creativity…for every marginal talent like the aforementioned artists, glam rock gave us gifts like David Bowie, T.Rex, Mott the Hoople, and the smoothest crooners of them all, Roxy Music.

Roxy Music's self-titled 1972 album made quite a splash even during the bloato-hyped glam rock era. Hitting Top Ten on the charts in the U.K. homeland, the band also received positive reviews stateside, so their sophomore effort – *For Your Pleasure* – was released in 1973 to some anticipation. The swansong for Brian Eno, who left the band afterwards to pursue a significant and influential solo career, *For Your Pleasure* featured elaborate production, complex yet melodic songs, and great performances from singer Bryan Ferry, guitarist Phil Manzanera, and multi-instrumentalist Andy MacKay, with electronic flourishes provided by Eno. Ferry made great leaps with his songwriting skills, delivering such cinematic masterpieces as "Do The Strand," "Strictly Confidential," and "In Every Dream Home A Heartache."

Warner Brothers' advertisement for the album was pitch-perfect, presenting the band as a bunch of glittery rock stars (with a rockabilly vibe) joyfully floating around the lay-out and surrounded by stars and glitter. Since the band was virtually unknown in the U.S. and was just breaking out in the U.K. (their debut album was a mere nine months earlier), so all the ad had to do was let people know that the album was available and maybe tickle the reader's curiosity…it worked for me and many others, as *For Your Pleasure* became the band's first charting album in the U.S. and was a #4 chart hit in the U.K.

Armand Schaubroeck's *Ratfucker* (1979)

As a rock 'n' roll obsessive living in the "Motor City" circa 1979-81, I attended a slew of record conventions in the city, searching for that *one* album that would make my collection. Held nearly every weekend *somewhere* in the Detroit area, the hardcore fan could scoop up rare 10" EPs, import albums, and bootleg discs from dozens of eager vendors. Rocker Armand Schaubroeck was an underground icon in the 'Rust Belt' during the late '70s, and it wasn't unusual to see his albums offered by the more adventuresome sellers. Usually compared with Lou Reed, Schaubroeck's band Armand Schaubroeck Steals eschewed Reed's NYC-centric 'heroin chic' in favor of a muscular, streetwise hard rock sound that often made Lou sound like a choirboy.

I picked up a copy of the band's debut album, *A Lot of People Would Like To See Armand Schaubroeck...Dead* at one such convention, an amazing triple-album set that warped my mind in ways still undiscovered. Schaubroeck was (and still is) the owner of the legendary House of Guitars store in Rochester, New York and was the proprietor of Mirror Records, through which he released his self-produced albums. No mere vanity imprint, Mirror also released albums by regional bands like Burning Orange, Dirty Looks, and their best-known act, Greg Prevost's legendary garage-rock outfit the Chesterfield Kings.

Since he ran the label, Schaubroeck ostensibly approved this *Trouser Press* ad, which is as raw and gritty and punkish as the music he made. With *Ratfucker*, his fourth and final album in the marquee position, the ad also lists all the other Armand Schaubroeck Steals albums as well as t-shirts. In the best tradition of Ralph Records, the ad includes Mirror Records' address (at the House of Guitars store) and encourages readers to write. Altogether a stunning and (hopefully) effective ad...now, if only those albums were reissued on CD...

Sire Records' "Don't Call It Punk" ad (1977)

Sire Records should be lauded for its free-thinking attitude towards new music in the late 1970s and early '80s. Formed in 1966 by industry veteran Seymour Stein (who made his bones with King Records) and songwriter/producer Richard Gottehrer, Sire Records quickly earned a reputation as an independent label with an eye on the underground, releasing albums by such diverse, non-mainstream artists as the Climax Blues Band, Matthews Southern Comfort, Focus, and the Deviants. Sensing changing trends in rock music in the late '70s, Stein signed the cream of the CBGB's crop to record deals, including bands like the Ramones, the Dead Boys, and Talking Heads.

Even after being swallowed whole by Warner Brothers Records in 1978, Stein ensured that Sire Records continued to sign a diverse range of artists, the label finding overwhelming mainstream success with acts like Madonna and the Pretenders, but also launching the careers of artists like the Flamin' Groovies, the Cure, the Smiths, and the Replacements. Sire was also an early player in rap music, releasing a handful of mid-to-late '80s era albums by Ice T.

This "Don't Call It Punk" advertisement from a 1977 issue of *Trouser Press* magazine is curiously and uncharacteristically tone-deaf for such a forward-thinking and progressive record label. Buying into the industry's overall attempt to whitewash punk rock by re-labeling it as "new wave," Sire went all-in by trying to hype its hot new albums – now-classic discs by Richard Hell & the Voidoids, Talking Heads, the Dead Boys, and the Saints – as the best of the "new wave," working hard to smooth the punk genre's rough edges and make it more commercially acceptable.

Three of the four albums featured are unabashedly punk in nature, and while I think that the ad's general lay-out and use of copy is effective, the label's futile attempt at downplaying what made these albums attractive to young listeners in the first place is laughable in light of the fact that three of these four discs have since become known as milestones of punk rock. So it goes...

Don't Call It Punk
If you're calling new rock & roll by the old name, you may need some wising up. Sire Records has some sound suggestions...

Richard Hell & The Voidoids
Blank Generation
One international music paper pronounced Hell "the future of American rock." His chilling "Blank Generation" serves as the anthem of the New Wave on both sides of the Atlantic. The writer-singer *Time* said "could become the Mick Jagger of punk" has been influential and idolized, all on his way to becoming one of the most magnetic 'stars' in contemporary music.

Talking Heads Talking Heads '77.
The *N.Y. Times* placed the fiery New York quartet "right at the top of the underground hierarchy." One critic gushed that the Heads were "the most intellectually interesting band I've heard anywhere in ages," while a devastating European tour and U.S. dates with Bryan Ferry enlisted still more believers. Full of flair, wit and superb rock & roll instincts, their debut album is destined to become a milestone.

Dead Boys
Young, Loud and Snotty.
Definitely not for the squeamish, Cleveland's Dead Boys exemplify the high tension end of the new rock & roll. High-strung and hell-bent, the Dead Boys proudly proclaim themselves hard rock partisans, stating their case with a vengeance on their first album.

The Saints
(I'm) Stranded
"We used to play the wildest songs we could find. Rock & roll is meant to be aggressive," claims Saints guitarist Ed Kuepper. The message hasn't been lost on British fans who made "(I'm) Stranded" *Sounds* magazine's No. 1 Single of 1976. The explosive hit kicks off one of the most furious albums ever.

From Sire Records, Inc., marketed by Warner Bros. Records Inc.

Stephen Stills & Manassas' *Down The Road* **(1972)**

Guitarist Stephen Stills already had enjoyed Rock & Roll Hall of Fame worthy stints with Buffalo Springfield and the 'supergroup' Crosby, Stills & Nash under his belt when he launched his solo career. After releasing a pair of commercially successful Top Ten solo albums – the first receiving mixed critical acclaim, the second rightfully deemed bloated and indulgent – Stills decided to get back into a band situation, forming Manassas with Chris Hillman of the Byrds/Flying Burrito Brothers and a roster of talented friends like steel guitarist Al Perkins (Flying Burrito Brothers) and CSN drummer Dallas Taylor, among others. The band's self-titled album performed respectively, rising to #4 on the *Billboard* chart and eventually certified for a Gold™ Record.

Whether you call 'em Manassas, or Stephen Stills' Manassas, as this Atlantic Records ad seems to label the band, there's no denying that its Stills' name at the top of the marquee (and other than Hillman, a talented musician who long suffered in the shadows of the more charismatic Roger McGuinn and Gram Parsons, the others weren't exactly household names to even the most fanatical rock consumer). Nevertheless, Atlantic's ad for the band's sophomore effort *Down The Road* is simplicity at its best (or worst) – just a bunch of hippies sitting around a table in the middle of a field somewhere.

The ad conveyed nothing about the music it represented, but presumably the audience for *Down The Road* were already familiar with Stills and Hillman's considerable musical pedigrees and didn't need a hard sell to coax them into buying the album. Although critically-slagged at the time as slight and inconsequential, in spite of guest turns by talents like Joe Walsh and Bobby Whitlock (Derek and the Dominos), *Down The Road* still managed to eke out a Top 30 ride on the charts, even if it fell short – critically and commercially – of its predecessor. Atlantic's ad campaign did the band (and the album) no favors…

10cc's *Bloody Tourists* (1978)

Quirky British art-rockers 10cc's best days were behind them when the 'other half' of the band – singer/guitarist Eric Stewart and singer/bassist Graham Gouldman – recorded 1978's *Bloody Tourists* with a line-up that included drummer Paul Burgess, guitarist Rick Fenn, and keyboardist Duncan Mackay. The two original band members had kept 10cc commercially relevant with their first album as a duo, the previous year's *Deceptive Bends*. Recorded in the wake of the departure of fellow songwriters Lol Crème and Kevin Godley, the album scored a surprise hit single with the Top Ten U.S. and U.K. hit "The Things We Do For Love."

The commercial fortunes of *Bloody Tourists* fell short of its predecessor in spite of the chart-topping U.K. hit "Dreadlock Holiday" (a funky slab o' reggae riddims that only climbed as high as #44 on the U.S. chart). The last album to be distributed in the states by Polydor Records (10cc would jump to Warner Brothers for 1980's *Look Hear?*), the label's advertising effort on behalf of the band isn't half bad. The image of the "bloody tourist" (geddit?) and bellboy is as quirky and oddball as anything the band had ever recorded, and the ad includes a list of tour dates and a picture of the album artwork to prompt consumers to look for it. Why do they call it "10cc's debut album on Polydor Records," though, when the band had been recording for Polydor subsidiary Mercury Records since its inception? 'Tis a mystery for the ages, perhaps...

Thee Image's *Thee Image* (1974)

Perhaps one of the more obscure bands offered in this book, Thee Image hasn't even merited its own Wikipedia entry in spite of having two fairly well-known musicians in its ranks in Mike Pinera and Duane Hitchings. Thee Image was formed in 1973 by singer and guitarist Pinera, who came to prominence with Blues Image (which enjoyed a #4 charting 1970 hit "Ride Captain Ride"), sat in for a hot minute with Iron Butterfly (contributing to their 1970 album *Metamorphosis*), and formed the short-lived Ramatam (two LPs) before joining Hitchings, a veteran of Buddy Miles' band, in the New Cactus Band. Hitchings, who had previously appeared on two Cactus albums – 1971's *Restrictions* and 1972's *'Ot N' Sweaty* – appropriated the band's name and, with Pinera, recorded one poorly-received album as the New Cactus Band without any of the guys that had made the band notable in the first place.

Pinera and Hitchings hooked up with drummer Donny Vosburgh (Pinera's former Blues Image bandmate) as Thee Image for a pair of mid-'70s albums. Signed to Emerson, Lake & Palmer's Manticore label (joining such commercial juggernauts as the power trio Stray Dog, King Crimson lyricist Pete Sinfield, and Italian proggers Premiate Forneria Marconi a/k/a PFM), Thee Image's self-titled debut album offered an innovative mix of hard and progressive rock that, while timed right, nevertheless failed to chart.

Manticore's advertisement for the album was both mesmerizing and effective, utilizing the album's checkerboard cover art motif behind a copy of the album cover itself, a photo of the band smaller than it needed to be, maybe, with the band members' credentials listed below. It was a striking graphic that did little to move units, and Thee Image would break up after the 1975 release of their second album, *Inside The Triangle*.

Mike Pinera. Duane Hitchings. Donny Vosburgh.
Bringing together the musical spark
from Iron Butterfly, Blues Image and Cactus
and creating an exciting new image.
Thee Image.

Rock and Roll Ballads from **Thee Image.**
brought to you by Manticore Records.

Distributed by Motown Record Corporation. © 1975, Manticore Records, Ltd.

Pete Townshend & Ronnie Lane's *Rough Mix* (1977)

Perhaps the most critically-acclaimed album of Who guitarist/songwriter Pete Townshend's storied solo career, much of the charm of *Rough Mix* can be attributed to the calming creative presence of former Small Faces and Faces' bassist Ronnie Lane. An underrated vocalist and a talented songwriter with an encyclopedic knowledge of American blues and country music and British folk, Lane was already fronting his genre-busting outfit Ronnie Lane's Slim Chance when he hooked up with his longtime friend Townshend to record *Rough Mix*, the album a bona fide rock 'n' roll classic that combined the best aspects of both artists on a fine collaborative effort.

Released stateside by MCA Records, the Who's label, any efforts to hype *Rough Mix* benefitted from the invaluable history of its two participants (as well as that of studio guests Eric Clapton and Who bassist John Entwistle). Thus the label did the minimum, creating a print ad that was a sort of cut 'n' paste of the cover artwork, blowing up a photo of the two artists to fill the frame and centering the album cover in the middle with Townshend and Lane's named writ large at the top. It was simple, tho' effective, announcing the album's release without saying much of the acoustic and electric folk-rock offering in the grooves. Then again, given the artists' image, perhaps MCA didn't need to do much more.

T.Rex's *Tanx* (1973)

Although the glam rock era of the early '70s was still raging in 1973, the shooting star that was Marc Bolan's T.Rex seemed to be plummeting to earth with the release of *Tanx*. While T.Rex's 1971 album *Electric Warrior* had provided Bolan his commercial breakthrough in the U.S. with the hit single "Bang A Gong (Get It On)," the following year's *The Slider* also brought critical acclaim along with chart success based on an enduring brace of songs in "Telegram Sam," "Metal Guru," and "Buick Mackane." *Tanx* had a lot to live up to after back-to-back hit albums, and while it performed admirably in the U.K. (peaking at #4), it faltered badly stateside, taking a major step backwards and only inching its way to #102 on the *Billboard* charts.

The advertising artwork created by Bolan's U.S. label Reprise Records (Frank Sinatra's boutique imprint) did absolutely nothing to boost T.Rex's chances with *Tanx*. Playing off the album artwork presumably created by EMI Records, who released the album in the U.K., Reprise emphasized the phallic aspects of the original cover artwork without adding anything of value to the transformation. While the original cover artwork offered a glammed-up and sultry Bolan showing some skin, posing provocatively slightly beside a toy tank (*Tanx*, geddit?), the U.S. ad artwork tosses any nuance out the window and, using a different and more imposing photo of Bolan, places the tank jutting directly out of the artist's loins. It was crass, ineffective, and not at all capturing Bolan's evolving sound or the album's mix of rock, soul, and funk music.

On Reprise Records and Tapes   (poster included in album)

UFO's *No Heavy Petting* (1976)

British hard-rockers UFO began life as a psychedelic-tinged space-rock band before evolving rapidly from their confusing first two 'numbered' albums, a metamorphosis that began with 1974's *Phenomenon* and in full bloom by the time of the 1976 release of *No Heavy Petting*. My friend and colleague Martin Popoff said it best in his book *The Collector's Guide to Heavy Metal, Volume 1: The Seventies* when he wrote that *"No Heavy Petting* embraces it all, becoming comfortable at once with a number of sentiments, defining class by virtue of its timelessness, by its lack of dated '70s elements which could have rendered this album merely a magnificent museum piece."

In spite of their relative stateside obscurity, classic era UFO – as defined by band members Phil Mogg, Michael Schenker, Pete Way, and Andy Parker – would provide a musical template and influence on bands like Iron Maiden, Megadeth, Metallica, and Pearl Jam, among others.

I'm really not sure what the Chrysalis Records creative team was smoking/swallowing/snorting when they designed this advertisement for UFO's *No Heavy Petting* album, but it's horrible. The striking original Hipgnosis album artwork (the third LP cover the legendary designers did for the band) is utilized and neutered by its inane surroundings, the cartoonish lettering of the band's name and the portrayal of a stellar landscape littered with twinkling stars matched by poorly-written copy that does little to introduce the band's fifth album to new listeners on either side of the Atlantic.

No Heavy Petting took a major step backwards commercially after the #71 peak of its predecessor, *Force It*, the album a creative triumph nonetheless that prefaced the band's short late '70s run of modestly-successful chart albums.

Johnny Winter's *Still Alive & Well* (1973)

After the release of the *Johnny Winter And* album in 1970, blues-rock guitarist Johnny Winter retreated from the music biz to seek treatment for his increasingly debilitating heroin addiction. During the interim, his brother Edgar scored big with his *They Only Come Out At Night* album and the hit single "Frankenstein." A common refrain during Edgar's 1972 tour was "hey man, where's your brother?"

The elder Winter brother came roaring back in 1973 with his fifth studio album, *Still Alive & Well*, the album title both an answer to the question on everybody's mind as well as a statement of defiance. Working with his former bandmates Rick Derringer and Randy Jo Hobbs, Winter delivered a high-energy set of blues and roots-rock that included a handful of original songs by Winter and Derringer as well as classic covers like Big Bill Broonzy's "Rock Me Baby" and the Rolling Stones' "Let It Bleed." The Stones also contributed a new song, "Silver Train," for Winter to spin his magic on, and Winter's original "Too Much Seconal" is a bluesy warning about drug abuse. Derringer's "Cheap Tequila" is a fine twangy roots-rocker while the title track is a defiant musical statement tailor-made for Winter's slash 'n' burn fretwork.

Still Alive & Well performed admirably in spite of Columbia Records' bland advertising efforts. This ad for the album is little more than a photo outtake from the session that provided the cover artwork. Displaying, perhaps, Winter's undeniable albino chic, it says little of the guitarist's return after three years, or of his expanding musical palette. The album would peak at #22 on the *Billboard* magazine albums chart anyway, Winter's fans obviously excited about the guitarist's much-anticipated return.

Wishbone Ash's *Front Page News* (1977)

British hard rock legends Wishbone Ash have always had a love/hate relationship with U.S. music buyers. Although they've long enjoyed a loyal, if smallish stateside following that exists to this day, the band's commercial fortunes waxed and waned alarmingly quickly in the early '70s, and they've failed to chart an album since 1981 although they continue to tour and record today under the aegis of early member Andy Powell. Whereas the band's classic 1972 album *Argus* peaked at #3 on the U.K. charts, here in the US of A, 1973's *Wishbone Four* represents the band's apex on this side of the pond, hitting #44 on the Billboard album chart.

Although Wishbone Ash managed to hold onto their status as a Top 40 band – more or less – through the end of the decade in their homeland, they had lost their juice with American audiences by the 1977 release of *Front Page News*, one of the last of the band's albums to chart in the U.S. Part of this was due to the album's musical direction, which leaned more heavily towards folk-influenced soft rock and away from their signature twin-guitar hard rock and prog mix. Part of their ebbing American audience, however, was due to the truly gruesome cover artwork the album was saddled with by MCA Records.

Playing off the album's title, the graphic designer tried to capture the feel of a newspaper's style in the use of bold fonts to convey headline-worthy information, but the jumble of floating band member photos on the layout is disconcerting and seems to portray separation rather than a united band vision. The advertisement for the album compounded the insult, using the album artwork and even more wonky ad copy and fonts that said little about the music and a lot about the designer's lack of imagination.

BONUS TRACK!

Kansas' *Masque* (1975)

Major labels really had no idea how to promote bands in the early-to-mid '70s, and frequently let them tour and record and evolve beyond their debut album in order to give them time to find a sound and audience. For a lot of bands, though, album number three was where the rubber hit the highway, and if sales weren't showing a marked upwards bound, that would be the end of the road for a lot of rockers.

One of two albums released by Kansas in 1975 (the first being *Song For America*), *Masque* didn't chart as high as its predecessor (peaking at #70), but it hit the Gold™ Record mark faster, allowing the band another shot at the brass ring, which they grabbed with their Top Ten charting masterpiece *Leftoverture* the following year. *Masque* earned its modest success entirely through the band's talents, 'cause Kirshner's advertisement for the album is pretty middlin', using the grotesque (tho' intriguing) album artwork along with ad copy that has little to do with the band or its genre-defining prog-rock sound ("molten metal"? Really?)

Kansas:the band behind the"Masque"!

Kansas—six musicians who make up what has to be the touring-est band in the land. They lighted in the studio long enough to make a record that comes on like a molten metal, roundhouse punch.

"Masque"—in the tough tradition of their first two giant albums, "Kansas" and "Song for America."

Kansas' new album, "Masque." Undisguised rock power on Kirshner Records and Tapes. Distributed by CBS Records.

KANSAS
masque

including
It Takes A Woman's Love (To Make A Man)
All The World/Two Cents Worth
Child Of Innocence/Mysteries And Mayhem

BONUS TRACK!

Ted Nugent's *Ted Nugent* (1975)

"Terrible" Ted Nugent had already achieved notoriety by the time of the release of his bona fide self-titled solo debut in 1975. Nugent's teen outfit the Amboy Dukes scored an enduring hit with "Journey To The Center of The Mind," the song living on via compilations of '60s psychedelic and garage-rock. Ted Nugent & the Amboy Dukes – featuring an entirely different line-up than the band's '60s-era roster – released a pair of solid, hard-rockin' albums in 1973 and '74 in *Call of The Wild* and *Tooth Fang & Claw* (for Frank Zappa's Bizarre label, no less), but Nugent's march to infamy began with this debut album.

This mini-ad for the album uses the ad copy and a small photo of the cover artwork to try and convey the energy of the music within without actually mentioning manic tunes like "Stranglehold," "Stormtroopin'," and "Motor City Madhouse." The advertising effort was mostly successful as the album went Top 30, but the lion's share of its success should be attributed to Nugent and his gang, who barnstormed across America, touring in support of the LP. Ted would receive better ad design with future releases like *Free-For-All* and *Cat Scratch Fever*.

Ted Nugent. Some claim he invented high energy. All agree he does it best. With his music, his songs and his very plugged-in guitar, Ted Nugent's new album entitled, modestly enough, "Ted Nugent," raises the threshold of high-energy rock and roll. **"Ted Nugent". High quality, high volume, high energy. On Epic Records and Tapes.**

Made in the USA
Monee, IL
17 August 2022

11869190R00056